AF263701

JACOBEE AND THE SCOUT PATROL

Frannie Laurie

Jacobee is my name,
Collecting honey is my game.

I have a question just for you.
If you can answer, oh please do!

What lays the most eggs a day?
If you know, will you say?

It's not a chicken or a duck.
It doesn't quack or even cluck.
I cluck
I quack

Let me tell you what I mean.
The answer is our very own Queen!

2,000 eggs a day she lays,
To attend to her needs, she must have maids.

Then one day they told the Queen,
Our supply of honey is very lean.

She then called for the Scout Patrol.
But where their leader was, they did not know.

The Queen ordered every Scout,
"Search here and there and round-about".

"We must have nectar for our hive,
And pollen too, so we can thrive!"

"The winner of this special quest,
Will be rewarded for doing best!"

Off they flew, they must make haste.
Flying here and there, not a minute to waste!

The Scouts came back by end-of-day,
From every direction with much to say.

They each came up and took a turn,
To share with the hive what they had learned.

To find the honey not by chance,
The Bees speak through the *Waggle Dance!*

Then it was time for Jacobee,
To do his dance for all to see.

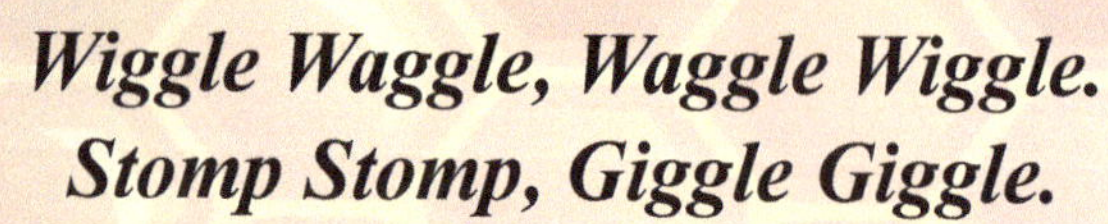

Wiggle Waggle, Waggle Wiggle.
Stomp Stomp, Giggle Giggle.

Left turn, Right turn,
Honey Bee Hop.
Right turn, Left turn,
Time to Stop!

The winner was plain to see,
None other than Jacobee!

The Queen announced to all the hive,
"Because of Jacobee, they would survive!"

As a reward, his new role,
Would be the leader of *THE SCOUT PATROL!!!*

THE END!

Hello friends, if you please,
Have some fun while helping Bees!

Plant some flowers and as you know,
This will help our hives to grow!